J. A Servizi, R. W Gordon, D. W Martens

Toxicity of two chlorinated catechols, possible components of kraft pulp mill bleach waste

J. A Servizi, R. W Gordon, D. W Martens

Toxicity of two chlorinated catechols, possible components of kraft pulp mill bleach waste

ISBN/EAN: 9783337714055

Printed in Europe, USA, Canada, Australia, Japan

Cover: Foto ©ninafisch / pixelio.de

More available books at **www.hansebooks.com**

INTERNATIONAL PACIFIC SALMON
FISHERIES COMMISSION

Appointed under a Convention
Between Canada and the United States for the
Protection, Preservation and Extension of
the Sockeye and Pink Salmon Fisheries
in the Fraser River System

PROGRESS REPORT

No. 17

TOXICITY OF TWO CHLORINATED CATECHOLS,
POSSIBLE COMPONENTS OF KRAFT PULP MILL BLEACH WASTE

By

J. A. Servizi, R. W. Gordon
and D. W. Martens

New Westminster, B.C.
Canada
1968

ABSTRACT

Young pink salmon were less tolerant of tetrachlorocatechol
than were sockeye. Advanced sockeye alevins were more tolerant
of tetrachlorocatechol than were freshly hatched alevins, fry or
smolts. Sublethal concentrations of di- and tetrachlorocatechol
caused an increase in respiration rate which, it is believed,
indicated disruption of cellular processes by uncoupling oxidative
phosphorylation. Tetrachlorocatechol was apparently oxidized by
biological treatment with activated sludge and it was concluded
that all chlorinated catechols and phenols, except pentachlorophenol,
would be oxidized by this treatment, if present in bleach waste.
Toxic strengths of chlorinated catechols and phenols were between
those of the non-chlorinated molecules and a common insecticide.
Application of the results was discussed in light of the possible
synergistic effects resulting from a mixture of chlorinated organic
compounds and other toxicants of industrial and domestic origin.

TABLE OF CONTENTS

TOXICITY OF TWO CHLORINATED CATECHOLS, POSSIBLE COMPONENTS OF KRAFT PULP MILL BLEACH WASTE*

INTRODUCTION

At present, three bleached kraft pulp mills are operating in the Fraser River watershed (FIGURE 1). The first mill, located at Kamloops, began operation in December, 1965, followed by two mills at Prince George which began operation in the spring and summer of 1966. A third mill is now under construction at Prince George while another is planned for Quesnel. Wastes produced by these mills are discharged, after treatment, to the Fraser and Thompson Rivers, both utilized as migration routes by major populations of juvenile and adult sockeye (Oncorhynchus nerka) and pink salmon (O. gorbuscha). Downstream segments of both rivers also serve as incubation areas for the majority of the pink salmon produced from the Fraser system. Kamloops Lake, located downstream from the Kamloops pulp mill, also serves as a sockeye rearing area. Elimination of toxic effects from mill wastes is thus vital to the protection of this valuable fishery resource.

Wastes produced by the mills, originating mainly from bleaching operations, are treated in biological treatment systems before being discharged, according to specifications drafted by regulatory agencies. Although biological treatment has effectively reduced acute toxicity of bleach wastes, further information is desired defining the toxicity of specific compounds in the wastes both before and after treatment. In order to fully understand possible ill effects of pulp mill discharges, even after treatment, lethal and sublethal levels of individual bleach waste toxicants should be determined. Through use of this knowledge, specifications and regulations can be developed which will assure that conditions safe

* This research was sponsored by the Governments of Canada and the United States with a part of the United States contribution originating from the Federal Water Pollution Control Administration of the U.S. Department of the Interior.

FIGURE 1 - Fraser River watershed showing the sites of present and proposed pulp mills on waterways serving as sockeye migration routes and pink salmon spawning areas.

for salmon are maintained, not only during brief exposure to
mill wastes, but also for the extended period that eggs, fry,
smolts and adults may be present within the Fraser River watershed.

A comprehensive analysis of bleach waste to determine its
toxic compounds has yet to be reported, although some interest in
this project has been expressed by a few analytical laboratories.
Since years may be required before these analyses are completed it
was believed wise to commence toxicity studies of compounds which
expert advice and previous research indicated might be present in
bleach waste. In the present study, acute toxicity of chlorinated
catechols, specifically di- and tetrachlorocatechol, was examined.
For comparative purposes, acute toxicities of di- and tetrachlorophenol
were also determined. The influence of chlorinated catechols on the
oxygen utilization rates of young sockeye and pink salmon was measured
to indicate the sublethal effects of these compounds. In addition,
the ability of biological treatment to oxidize tetrachlorocatechol was
examined.

ORIGIN AND POTENTIAL TOXIC ACTION OF CHLORINATED CATECHOLS

Lignin, along with cellulose and other carbohydrates, forms the
basic structure of wood. The purpose of pulping and bleaching is to
remove the lignin and carbohydrate while retaining the cellulose.
Carbohydrates, lignin and the products formed during their separation
from cellulose are carried in the pulp wastes. Those wastes produced
during pulping operations are removed within the mill while those
produced during bleaching operations are discharged.

Research has shown that lignin is aromatic in nature, possibly
being composed of phenylpropane and guaiacyl propane units (Sarkanen,
1963). Due to its aromatic structure one might expect that
chlorination of lignin during bleaching would result in formation of
various chlorinated aromatic compounds which would be carried in the
waste discharge. As the result of the various woods employed, and
the techniques and severity of bleaching, waste products may vary in
kind and concentration. For example, it has been suggested (Sarkanen,

personal communication) that chlorination of guaiacyl propane units may result in formation of di- and tetrachlorocatechol. A pictorial representation of the three compounds is presented below. The latter two compounds are broadly classified as chlorinated aromatic compounds and are in a category called polyhydric phenols or phenolic compounds.

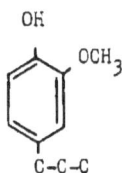

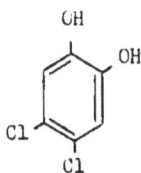

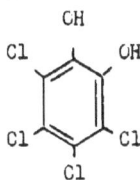

OH
OCH$_3$

C-C-C

OH
OH
Cl
Cl

OH
Cl
OH
Cl
Cl
Cl

guaiacyl propane unit   dichlorocatechol   tetrachlorocatechol

The toxicity of chlorinated catechols to fish has not been reported, but an indication of relative toxic strength to be expected can be deduced from comparisons with compounds of similar chemical structure. The chlorinated phenols, of which pentachlorophenol is the most widely known fish toxicant, are structurally similar to chlorinated catechols, as comparison of the following diagram with the previous one indicates.

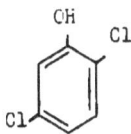

OH
Cl
Cl

OH
Cl
Cl
Cl
Cl
Cl

dichlorophenol   pentachlorophenol

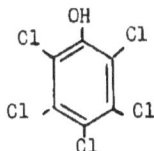

According to Sexton (1953), toxicity of phenolic compounds to bacteria depends upon the number of chlorine and hydroxyl groups on the molecule. He explained that toxicity increased as chlorine was added to a phenolic molecule, but that polyhydric phenols (such as catechol) were less toxic to bacteria than was phenol itself. It can be deduced from Sexton's generalizations that dichlorocatechol would be less toxic to fish than tetrachlorocatechol, and that the chlorinated catechols would be less toxic than the corresponding chlorinated phenol. Therefore, for comparative purposes, the acute toxicities of di- and

tetrachlorophenol were determined in the present study in addition to the toxicities of di- and tetrachlorocatechol.

The mechanism by which chlorinated catechols cause toxicity has not been reported, but a possible mode of action can be assumed from knowledge of the toxic action of the structurally similar compound, pentachlorophenol. Toxicity of pentachlorophenol results from its interference with phosphorylation processes in the living cell (White et al., 1959). This interference is termed "uncoupling of oxidative phosphorylation" and occurs when a substance enters a living cell and disrupts the flow of energy from "energy yielding" functions (e.g., oxidation of food) to "energy requiring" functions such as cell maintenance and synthesis. Uncouplers are quick acting toxicants and may cause death in a few minutes or hours at acutely toxic concentrations.

A symptom commonly associated with "uncoupling" is increased respiration (oxygen consumption) which occurs because the metabolic processes attempt to overcome a deficit in the flow of energy to those functions requiring it. Since tetrachlorocatechol is somewhat similar in chemical structure to pentachlorophenol, the possibility exists that it too may be an "uncoupler", in which case respiration rate of fish in contact with acute or subacute concentrations of tetrachlorocatechol would be increased. In order to test this possibility, respiration rates of young sockeye and pink salmon in contact with di- and tetrachlorocatechol were compared with normal respiration rates in water only.

It has been assumed that chlorinated catechols may be present in bleach waste. Since these wastes are oxidized in biological systems to reduce toxicity, it is logical to question whether chlorinated catechols may resist this treatment and be discharged to the receiving waters. Catechol can be oxidized during biological treatment (Malaney, 1960), but there is no report of the oxidation of chlorinated

catechols. However, an indication of the likelihood of successful biological oxidation of chlorinated catechols may be obtained by reference to oxidation of the structurally similar chlorinated phenols. Research has shown that biological treatment oxidized mono-, di- and trichlorophenol while pentachlorophenol was resistant (Ingols, Gaffney and Stevenson, 1966). Based upon these data, and the fact that catechol itself can be oxidized, it is likely that dichlorocatechol would be oxidized during biological treatment. The fate of tetrachlorocatechol cannot be so easily estimated and was determined experimentally in the present study.

MATERIALS AND METHODS

Sources of Fish

Pink and sockeye salmon used in the present experiments were obtained from various sources. All sockeye were of the Cultus Lake or Pitt River races. Some Cultus Lake sockeye alevins were incubated in the Cultus Lake hatchery while others originated from naturally spawned stock. The latter alevins were dug from redds on the Lindell Beach spawning ground of Cultus Lake. Sockeye smolts were trapped in Sweltzer Creek during their seaward migration from Cultus Lake. Pitt River sockeye fry were reared in outdoor ponds at Cultus Lake hatchery following transfer from an incubation channel at Pitt River.

The pink salmon alevins used in the present tests originated from Skeena River (courtesy Department of Fisheries of Canada) and from Sweltzer Creek. Both stocks were hatchery incubated. Pink salmon fry were obtained during migration from an incubation channel used by Sweltzer Creek stocks.

The origin of fish used in each test is restated where applicable in the RESULTS.

Reagents

Di- and tetrachlorocatechol were supplied through courtesy of
Dr. K.V. Sarkanen, Institute of Forest Products, University of
Washington. Tetrachlorophenol was Eastman Technical Grade while
2,5-dichlorophenol was Eastman Grade.

Tests of Acute Toxicity

Acute (lethal) toxicity of di- and tetrachlorocatechol to young
pink and sockeye salmon was measured in 96-hr and 31-day bioassays.
In addition, the acute toxicities of di- and tetrachlorophenol to
sockeye fry during 96-hr exposures were determined for comparison
with toxicity of the chlorinated catechols. Bioassays using bleach
waste were of 96-hr duration.

Ninety-six Hour Exposure

Short-term exposure (96 hr) of fish to toxic materials was
carried out in standing-water bioassays using plastic aquaria of
1- to 10-liter capacity. Five to 10 fish were used in each test
and concentrations of fish ranged from 0.3 to 3.9 gm per liter
(TABLE 1). Cultus Lake water was used and dissolved oxygen was
kept near saturation with compressed air.

TABLE 1 - Concentrations of fish in short-term bioassays.

TEST SPECIMENS AND TOXICANT	AQUARIA VOLUME liters	NUMBER OF FISH	CONCENTRATION OF FISH	
			No./liter	gm/liter
Chlorinated Catechols and Phenols:				
Sockeye alevins, freshly hatched	1	5	5	0.3
Sockeye alevins, advanced size	1	5	5	0.6
Sockeye fry, 55 mm long	10	10	1	2.0
Sockeye fry, 42 mm long	10	10	1	0.8
Sockeye smolts, 85 mm long	8	5	0.6	3.9
Pink salmon alevins	1	5	5	1.0
Pink salmon fry	1	5	5	1.3
Neutralized bleach waste:				
Sockeye fry, 42 mm long	3	5	1.67	1.3

The 96-hr median tolerance limit (96-hr TL_m), representing the concentration of a toxicant which will kill 50 per cent of the fish in 96 hr, was used as a measure of acute toxicity. In order to determine 96-hr TL_m, several concentrations of the substance being tested were prepared using Cultus Lake water, test fish were added, and mortalities removed each 24 hr. The 96-hr TL_m was determined by plotting per cent concentration versus per cent survivors after 96 hr on semilogarithmic paper and drawing a straight line between two points which had survivals greater than 50 per cent, and less than 50 per cent, respectively. The concentration which corresponded to 50 per cent survival on this line was the median tolerance limit (Henderson and Tarzwell, 1957).

Fish were bioassayed at the temperature of the water from which they were taken. Temperature was controlled by standing the aquaria in constant-flow water baths. Smolts were held overnight, following capture, in aquaria before use in a bioassay. Fry and smolts were not fed during or for 24 hr before a bioassay. All control fish survived short-term bioassays in good condition.

Thirty-one Day Exposure

Flowing-water bioassays with sockeye alevins and fry were performed using concentrations of 0.6, 0.2, 0.1, 0.05 ppm tetrachlorocatechol and 0.2 ppm dichlorocatechol, respectively, in five experimental troughs plus three control troughs. Troughs were covered to exclude light during the alevin stage but were uncovered as the fish advanced to the "swim-up" fry stage. The troughs measured 59.5 in. by 5.25 in. by 7 in. deep with a water detention time of 1.6 hr. In each trough, fish were held in four plastic screen baskets measuring 6 in. by 5.25 in. by 6 in. deep. The first three baskets per trough, each containing 120 fish of identical age and origin, were considered a single group (Group 1). The fourth basket, Group 2, contained 140 fish which were less developed than those in Group 1. Temperatures were maintained at 45°F throughout the experiment.

Constant concentrations of di- and tetrachlorocatechol were maintained by metering fresh Cultus Lake water and a 25-ppm solution of the respective toxicant into the troughs using overflow plastic headboxes. Water and solutions were well mixed by introduction of compressed air through air stones at the inlet end of the troughs. Dissolved oxygen was near saturation (12 ppm).

Alevins in Groups 1 and 2 were hatchery-incubated Cultus Lake race sockeye. The fish in Groups 1 and 2 were taken from hatchery baskets and acclimated to the apparatus for eight and six days, respectively, before the test solutions were introduced. No mortalities occurred during the acclimation period. Group 1 alevins were further advanced than those in Group 2 and at the time that the test solutions were introduced to the troughs they had accumulated 1,500 and 1,300 temperature units, respectively. Fish in Group 1 reached the "swim-up" fry stage about 14 days after addition of the test solution while those in Group 2 required 29 days. Exposure to toxicant was continuous for 31 days for each group: Group 1 for 14 days as alevins and 17 days as fry, and Group 2 for 29 days as alevins and two days as fry. Fry were fed Abernathy dry diet,[1] in excess, eight times per day commencing at "swim-up".

Measurements of Respiration Rate

The effect of chlorinated catechols on respiration rate was determined by comparing oxygen consumption of experimental and control groups of young sockeye and pink salmon during a 5-hr period. Prior to testing, fish were held overnight in one liter plastic aquaria in the same concentration of di- or tetrachlorocatechol at which they were to be tested the next day, except in a few cases described in the RESULTS. Fish were held and tested at the temperature of the water from which they were taken. Fry were not fed for 48 hr before testing.

---

[1] Developed at the U.S. Fish and Wildlife Service Salmon Cultural Laboratory, Abernathy Creek, Longview, Washington.

Fish were transferred from the aquaria to darkened glass test bottles, in seconds, by gently pouring them onto a plastic screen to remove water and then pouring them through a funnel made from a piece of plastic screen into the bottle. Five fish were put into 525-ml bottles and 10 to 20 fish in 1,050-ml bottles. The bottles were sealed and immersed on their sides in a darkened constant-temperature bath. In any one experimental trial, concentrations of fish were identical and are noted in the RESULTS.

Before fish were added, the bottles were filled with Cultus Lake water drawn from a 30-liter aquarium which was aerated for 30 min to bring it to equilibrium. Chlorinated catechol was added to bottles from a well aerated 25-ppm stock solution. No chlorinated catechol was added to bottles meant for control fish. In addition, two blank samples containing water only and two reagent blanks containing water and chlorinated catechol were treated similarly to those bottles containing fish.

After the 5-hr test period, water was siphoned from each test bottle into a 300-ml BOD bottle and dissolved oxygen was measured by the Azide modification of the Winkler method (Standard Methods, 1965). Comparison of dissolved oxygen in reagent and sample blanks at the end of the test with dissolved oxygen in the aquarium at the start indicated no change in oxygen concentration had occurred. The difference between dissolved oxygen in blanks and that in controls or experimental bottles was the amount of oxygen used by the fish and usually varied between 1 and 2 ppm. Respiration rate was calculated as the milligrams of oxygen utilized per hour per gram of dry weight of alevin body or fry. Relative respiration rate was the ratio of respiration rate of experimental to control fish.

Fish were preserved in 10 per cent formalin upon completion of each experiment. Alevin bodies were separated from yolks by careful dissection before being weighed. Fry, alevin bodies, and yolks were dried at 98°C for 24 hr and dry weights were determined on an automatic analytical balance accurate to 0.01 mg.

Biological Treatment of Bleach Waste
Containing Added Chlorinated Catechol

In order to determine whether tetrachlorocatechol would be
oxidized during biological treatment, a known amount of this
compound was added to bleach waste undergoing biological treatment.
The mixture was then bioassayed to evaluate tetrachlorocatechol
oxidation.

The bleach waste mixture used in these experiments was
obtained from a kraft pulp mill when the mill was making full
bleach pulp (brightness 89 to 92) from coniferous trees. The
mixture consisted of the following components; caustic bleach
waste (24.4 per cent), acid bleach waste (36.6 per cent) and wash
water from the final washing of pulp following recovery of black
liquor (39 per cent). This mixture was very acid, having a pH of
about 3, but before use in treatment or bioassay it was neutralized
to pH 7 to 7.4 with 10N KOH (Servizi, Stone and Gordon, 1966).

An activated sludge (heterogeneous bacterial culture) was
developed on neutralized bleach waste (NBW) by aerating a mixture
of 4 liters domestic sewage, 4 liters NBW and 200 ml of soil
elutriate for two successive 24-hr periods separated by settling
of sludge and re-feeding. After initial development of sludge,
settling and re-feeding were continued for a week at 24-hr intervals
with NBW as the sole organic source. Sludge was supplied with
nitrogen and phosphorous throughout the acclimation and experimental
periods at the rate of BOD/N/P equal to approximately 200/10/1.

Following acclimation, 400 ml of settled acclimated sludge was
separated into two equal portions and 4 liters of NBW was added to
one portion while 4 liters of NBW with 3 ppm tetrachlorocatechol
added was fed to the other portion. The two mixtures were aerated
for 24 hr and then settled. Enough supernatant was drawn off for a

96-hr bioassay and aeration was then continued for four additional days, making a total treatment of five days for the remaining waste. Sludge was settled and supernatant decanted for acute toxicity bioassay after five days of treatment.

RESULTS

Acute Toxicity of Chlorinated Catechols

Ninety-six Hour Exposure

Tetrachlorocatechol was found toxic to sockeye alevins, fry and smolts at low concentrations. The 96-hr TL_m of newly hatched natural and hatchery-incubated sockeye alevins (body weights approximately 10 mg) to tetrachlorocatechol was 0.7 ppm (TABLE 2). In contrast to the freshly hatched alevins, the 96-hr TL_m's of advanced hatchery alevins (body weights 15 and 18 mg) were 1.1 and 1.3 ppm. The 96-hr TL_m's of sockeye fry from Cultus hatchery and Pitt Lake incubation channel were 0.8 and 0.9 ppm, respectively. Natural sockeye smolts had a 96-hr TL_m of 0.8 ppm. The foregoing data indicate that natural smolts, freshly hatched natural and hatchery alevins, hatchery fry and incubation channel fry were about equally susceptible to tetrachlorocatechol while advanced sockeye alevins appeared somewhat more resistant.

Pink salmon alevins and fry had 96-hr TL_m's of 0.29 and 0.26 ppm, respectively (TABLE 2). These results showed that in the early life stages pink salmon were more susceptible to tetrachlorocatechol than were sockeye.

Dichlorocatechol was less toxic to sockeye and pink salmon than was tetrachlorocatechol. The 96-hr TL_m ranged from 2.4 to 2.7 ppm for sockeye advanced alevins and fry, respectively (TABLE 3). In contrast to results obtained with tetrachlorocatechol, advanced pink salmon alevins (96-hr TL_m of 2.0 ppm) were almost as tolerant of dichlorocatechol as were sockeye.

TABLE 2 - Acute toxicity of tetrachlorocatechol to sockeye and pink salmon expressed as 96-hr median tolerance limit (96-hr TL_m).

SPECIES, STAGE OF DEVELOPMENT AND SOURCE	SIZE OF TEST FISH			TEMP. $^\circ F$	96-HR TL_m ppm
	Dry weight, mg		Fork Length mm		
	Alevin Body	Yolk			
SOCKEYE SALMON.					
Alevins - Newly Hatched					
Cultus - Hatchery	(9)	(18)		41	0.7
Cultus - Natural	(9)	(18)		46	0.7
Alevins - Advanced					
Cultus - Hatchery	15	11		41	1.1
Cultus - Hatchery	18	10		41	1.3
Fry					
Cultus - Hatchery			55	49	0.8
Pitt - Incubation Channel			42	49	0.9
Smolt - Yearling					
Cultus - Natural			85	47	0.8
PINK SALMON:					
Alevins - Advanced					
Sweltzer - Hatchery	25	29		41	0.29
Sweltzer - Hatchery	25	29		41	0.29
Fry					
Sweltzer - Incubation Channel			35	46	0.26

( ) Approximate values from Brannon (1965).

TABLE 3 - Acute toxicity of dichlorocatechol to sockeye and pink salmon expressed as 96-hr median tolerance limit (96-hr TL_m).

SPECIES, STAGE OF DEVELOPMENT AND SOURCE	SIZE OF TEST FISH			TEMP. °F	96-HR TL_m ppm
	Dry Weight, mg		Fork Length mm		
	Alevin Body	Yolk			
SOCKEYE SALMON.					
Alevins - Advanced					
Cultus - Hatchery	17	10		41	2.4
Fry					
Pitt - Incubation Channel			42	48	2.7
PINK SALMON.					
Alevins - Advanced					
Sweltzer - Hatchery	25	29		41	2.0

The difference between those concentrations of di- and tetrachlorocatechol causing 100 per cent mortality in 96 hr and those causing little or no mortality was small. For example, 1.0 ppm tetrachlorocatechol killed 100 per cent of freshly hatched sockeye alevins while none were killed at 0.5 ppm. In addition, all advanced pink salmon alevins were killed at 0.375 ppm tetrachlorocatechol, while only 20 per cent succumbed at 0.25 ppm and all survived at 0.175 ppm. Similarly, 3.0 ppm dichlorocatechol killed 90 per cent of sockeye fry (42 mm fork length) while none were killed at 2.5 ppm. Fifty per cent of advanced pink alevins were killed at 2.0 ppm dichlorocatechol but none died at 1.0 ppm.

Thirty-one Day Exposure

During the 31-day exposure to chlorinated catechols, fish in Group 1 progressed from the alevin into the fry stage, 14 days in the former and 17 days in the latter. Fish in Group 2 were at a less advanced stage of development at the start of the bioassay and spent 29 days as alevins and two as fry in contact with tetra- or dichlorocatechol.

Mortalities of sockeye alevins exposed to 0.6 ppm tetrachlorocatechol were 79 and 76 per cent in Groups 1 and 2, respectively, after nine days (TABLE 4). Fish remaining alive after nine days in 0.6 ppm tetrachlorocatechol were severely distressed, some being moribund, so this concentration was discontinued in order to conserve reagent which was in short supply. The bulk of the mortalities in both groups occurred primarily during a 48-hr interval from the seventh to the ninth days of exposure. No significant mortalities occurred at tetrachlorocatechol concentrations of 0.2, 0.1 or 0.06 ppm.

At 0.2 ppm dichlorocatechol (TABLE 4), no mortalities were recorded among either group tested. Unfortunately, higher concentrations of dichlorocatechol could not be tested without exhausting supplies required for other experiments.

With the exception of fish exposed to 0.6 ppm tetrachlorocatechol, all surviving alevins apparently progressed normally to the fry stage and readily accepted food.

Acute Toxicity of Chlorinated Phenols

The chlorinated phenols were found to be more toxic than the respective catechols. The 96-hr TL_m's of tetra- and dichlorophenol were 0.48 and 1.7 ppm, respectively, for sockeye fry from Pitt Lake incubation channel. That is, tetra- and dichlorophenol were about 1.8 and 1.6 times as toxic, respectively, as the corresponding catechol.

TABLE 4 - Mortality of sockeye alevins and fry (Cultus race, hatchery reared) continuously exposed to tetrachlorocatechol and dichlorocatechol at 45°F. Original numbers of fish in Groups 1 and 2 were 360 and 140, respectively.

REAGENT CONC. ppm	GROUP TESTED	ALEVINS			FRY			TOTAL		
		Exposure days	Mortality NO.	%	Exposure days	Mortality NO.	%	Exposure days	Mortality No.	%
Tetrachlorocatechol										
0.6	1	9*	285	79.2				9	285	79.2
	2	9*	107	76.4				9	107	76.4
0.2	1	14	-	-	17	3	0.8	31	3	0.8
	2	29	-	-	2	-	-	31	-	-
0.1	1	14	-	-	17	-	-	31	-	-
	2	29	5	3.6	2	-	-	31	5	3.6
0.05	1	14	-	-	17	-	-	31	-	-
	2	29	-	-	2	-	-	31	-	-
Dichlorocatechol										
0.2	1	14	-	-	17	-	-	31	-	-
	2	29	-	-	2	-	-	31	-	-
Controls										
0.0	1	14	-	-	17	-	-	31	-	-
	1	14	-	-	17	5	1.4	31	5	1.4
	1	14	-	-	17	-	-	31	-	-
	2	29	-	-	2	-	-	31	-	-
	2	29	2	1.4	2	-	-	31	2	1.4
	2	29	2	1.4	2	-	-	31	2	1.4

* Mortality occured in first nine days, remaining fish distressed, experiment halted.

As with the chlorinated catechols, there was only a small difference between the concentration of chlorinated phenol which caused 100 per cent mortality and that which caused none during 96-hr exposure of sockeye fry from Pitt Lake incubation channel. Tetrachlorophenol caused 100 per cent mortality at 0.50 ppm and none at 0.45 ppm while comparable figures for dichlorophenol were 1.8 and 1.5 ppm.

Condition and Behavior of Test Fish

All fish tested appeared outwardly to be in good condition. Behavior of experimental and control fish was observed during all bioassays and the only outward symptom of toxicity noted was loss of equilibrium several hours before death. In general, those fish which survived bioassays behaved as the control fish did. Pink salmon fry were especially excitable, possibly due to their urge to migrate, and the level of activity in both control and experimental aquaria was high. However, it was concluded that observable activity of pink and sockeye was independent of tetra- or dichlorocatechol concentration at sublethal levels.

Effect of Chlorinated Catechols on Respiration

Sockeye Salmon Alevins

Measurements indicated that sublethal concentrations of tetrachlorocatechol caused increased oxygen utilization (respiration rate) by sockeye salmon alevins. The relative respiration rate of hatchery-incubated Cultus Lake sockeye alevins in 0.75 ppm tetrachlorocatechol was 1.61, indicating a 61 per cent increase in respiration over the control rate (TABLE 5, Trial A). The relative rate decreased as concentration of tetrachlorocatechol was reduced so that at 0.125 ppm the respiration rate was only seven per cent greater than that of the controls. The results represent samples of 20 alevins at each concentration and in each of the two controls.

TABLE 5 - Respiration rate of sockeye salmon alevins in tetrachlorocatechol (TCC); five alevins per 525-ml bottle, except where noted.

TRIAL AND TEMP. °F	STOCK	ALEVIN MEAN DRY WEIGHT, mg		CONC. TCC ppm	RATE OF OXYGEN UTILIZATION, mg O$_2$/hr/gm		
		Body	Yolk		Individual Tests	Mean for Each Conc.	Relative Rate Expt./Control
A[a] 40.8	Hatchery Cultus Race	17.65	9.50	Control	1.227	1.223	1.00
		17.33	9.44	Control	1.219		
		16.34	9.64	0.75	1.969	1.969	1.61
		16.14	9.49	0.50	1.667	1.667	1.36
		17.07	9.99	0.25	1.422	1.422	1.16
		16.54	8.94	0.125	1.311	1.311	1.07
B 44.4	Natural Spawn Cultus Race	15.11	12.25	Control	1.237	1.118	1.00
		15.61	11.97	Control	1.000		
		13.72	13.23	0.75	1.825	1.686	1.51
		14.84	12.41	0.75	1.547		
		14.45	12.48	0.40	1.010	1.147	1.03
		13.78	13.76	0.40	1.284		
C 48.2	Natural Spawn Cultus Race	15.50	2.47	Control	1.853	2.096	1.00
		16.12	3.09	Control	2.340		
		16.20	2.62	0.75	1 mortality	-	
		15.19	4.10	0.75	1 mortality		
		14.63	3.35	0.55	2.500	2.455	1.17
		14.77	4.92	0.55	2.410		
		14.90	3.64	0.30	2.245	2.140	1.02
		15.45	3.82	0.30	2.035		
D 48.2	Same alevins as C identify by weights	16.20	2.62	Control	2.150	1.992[b]	
		15.19	4.10	Control	1.835		
		14.63	3.35	Control	1.965	2.118[b]	1.00
		14.77	4.92	Control	2.270		
		14.90	3.64	Control	1.965	1.998[b]	
		15.45	3.82	Control	2.030		
		15.50	2.47	0.55	2.700	2.712	1.33
		16.12	3.09	0.55	2.725		

[a] Twenty alevins in 1,050-ml bottles.

[b] Average of these three figures is 2.036.

Several respiration rate measurements were made using alevins dug from the natural spawning ground at Cultus Lake. At 0.75 and 0.40 ppm of tetrachlorocatechol, relative respiration rates were 1.51 and 1.03, respectively, in Trial B (TABLE 5). Two alevins died at 0.75 ppm tetrachlorocatechol in Trial C. These were the only mortalities associated with measurements of respiration rate and probably occurred because 0.75 ppm was near the lethal level for sockeye alevins. Relative respiration rates at 0.55 and 0.30 ppm tetrachlorocatechol were 1.17 and 1.02, respectively in Trial C.

Alevins from Trial C were retested the following day in Trial D except that conditions were reversed. That is, control alevins from Trial C were tested at 0.55 ppm tetrachlorocatechol after overnight exposure to that concentration, whereas those alevins subjected to tetrachlorocatechol in Trial C were held in fresh water and served as controls in Trial D. The Trial C control alevins showed a 29 per cent increase in respiration rate when tested in 0.55 ppm tetrachlorocatechol in Trial D (2.712 versus 2.096). Furthermore, alevins transferred to fresh water from tetrachlorocatechol for Trial D had an average respiration rate similar to that for controls on the previous day (2.036 versus 2.096), indicating apparent return to normal respiration. Comparison of average respiration rate of the alevins tested at 0.30 ppm tetrachlorocatechol in Trial C (2.140) with their average respiration rate in fresh water the following day (1.998) indicated respiration rate under experimental conditions was seven per cent greater than under control conditions. A similar comparison with alevins at 0.55 ppm tetrachlorocatechol indicated respiration rate under experimental conditions (Trial C) was 16 per cent greater (2.455 versus 2.118) than under control conditions (Trial D).

Average relative respiration rates of naturally spawned alevins were calculated for each tetrachlorocatechol concentration from

relative respiration rates shown in TABLE 5 and were plotted in
FIGURE 2. Over the range of concentrations tested it appeared
that relative respiration was proportional to tetrachlorocatechol
concentration. However, average respiration rates of naturally
spawned alevins decreased faster than those of hatchery alevins as
tetrachlorocatechol concentrations decreased. The difference in
slope of the data for natural and hatchery alevins may have been
related to incubation conditions, alevin size, or temperature.
Note that bodies of hatchery alevins used in Trial A were a little
larger than those in the other trials. Furthermore, alevins from
natural spawn used in Trial B were slightly smaller than those in
Trials C and D but there was a large difference in the amount of
yolk remaining. Since these alevins were obtained from the same
spawning area, a difference in egg size or natural incubation
conditions may have influenced development. Temperature has a
marked effect upon respiration rate, but in order for it to affect
relative respiration rate it would have required that temperature
not have a parallel effect on respiration of test and control fish.
Further research would be required to define the importance of
these various factors.

The data in TABLE 5 and FIGURE 2 do not permit precise estimates
of the lowest concentrations of tetrachlorocatechol at which
respiration rate was increased and further experimental work would
be required in order to make these estimates. However, the
accumulated data suggest that respiration of the hatchery and natural
alevins was accelerated at concentrations greater than 0.1 and 0.3 ppm
tetrachlorocatechol, respectively.

In order to confirm that dichlorocatechol would act on salmon in
the same manner as tetrachlorocatechol, the relative respiration rate
of hatchery-incubated Cultus Lake sockeye alevins (similar to Trial A)
was determined at a single concentration using duplicate samples of

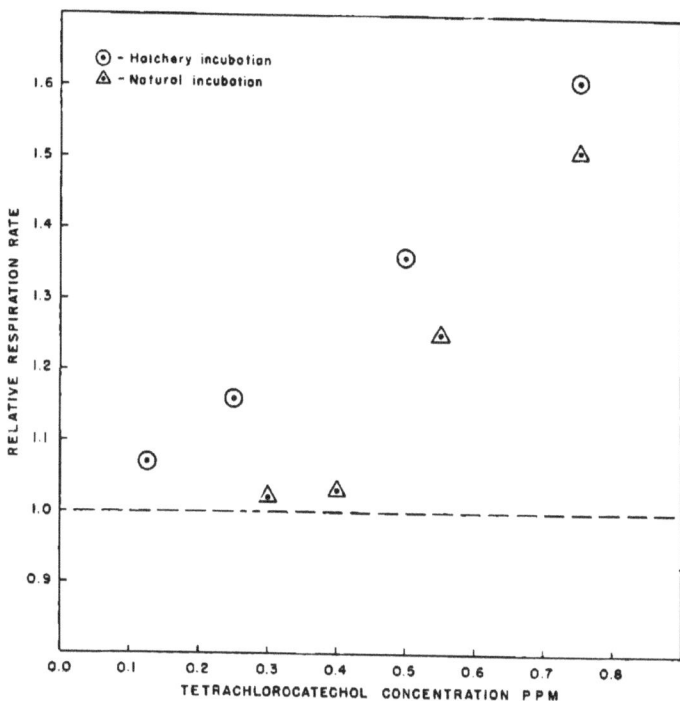

FIGURE 2 – Respiration rate (rate of oxygen utilization) of sockeye salmon alevins in tetrachlorocatechol relative to controls. Cultus Lake stock, hatchery and natural incubation.

10 alevins each at 42°F. Respiration rates of control alevins were 0.110 and 0.183 mg/hr/gm while respiration rates of alevins at 1.5 ppm dichlorocatechol were 0.189 and 0.198 mg/hr/gm. The average relative respiration rate was calculated as 1.32 from these data. Thus it is seen that dichlorocatechol also caused an increase in respiration rate but required a concentration which was approximately three times as great as that of tetrachlorocatechol to produce the same response.

Sockeye Salmon Fry

Measurements of respiration rates of sockeye fry were made at tetrachlorocatechol concentrations between 0.05 and 0.40 ppm in an attempt to define the minimum concentration at which tetrachlorocatechol would affect respiration. Respiration rates of the two control groups of fry varied widely between 1.165 and 1.940 mg O_2/hr/gm (TABLE 6). Except for one group, the respiration rates of experimental fry were between those for the two control samples. This condition arose, it is believed, from variation in activity of fry in the bottles. Observations of fry held in conditions similar to those in the experiment, except that light was not excluded, indicated that degree of activity was independent of sublethal concentrations of tetrachlorocatechol but was influenced by activity of individual fish. For example, in some of the control and experimental bottles, a single fry swam vigorously much of the time and this seemed to increase the general level of activity in the group. As a result, fry in some bottles were undoubtedly more active than in others and this difference in activity would have caused variations in oxygen consumption unrelated to tetrachlorocatechol concentration (Brett, 1962).

The average relative respiration rates were 1.04, 1.27 and 1.05 for fry held overnight in tetrachlorocatechol and tested at 0.2, 0.1 and 0.05 ppm, respectively (TABLE 6). For fry held overnight in water only, respiration rates measured in tetrachlorocatechol were 1.13 and

23

1.10 at 0.40 ppm and 0.20 ppm. The results suggested that
tetrachlorocatechol caused increased respiration rate, possibly at
concentrations as low as 0.1 ppm, but a consistent direct
relationship to tetrachlorocatechol concentration was not evident.
Had higher concentrations of tetrachlorocatechol been used (about
0.7 ppm), more positive results might have been obtained. Lack of
a direct relationship was probably related to differences in activity
of fry in the various bottles, as already discussed. Further
measurements of respiration rate using fry would require a
respirometer in which activity could be controlled in order to
eliminate it as a variable.

TABLE 6 - Respiration rate of sockeye salmon fry in tetrachlorocatechol
(TCC); five fry per 525-ml bottle.

TRIAL AND TEMP. °F	STOCK	FRY MEAN DRY WEIGHT mg	CONC. TCC ppm	RATE OF OXYGEN UTILIZATION, mg O_2/hr/gm		
				Individual Tests	Mean for Each Conc.	Relative Rate Expt./Control
E 45.0	Hatchery, Cultus Race	19.46	Control	1.940	1.552	1.00
		18.57	Control	1.165		
		21.18	0.20	1.630	1.618	1.04
		21.54	0.20	1.605		
		18.90	0.10	2.110	1.973	1.27
		18.96	0.10	1.836		
		18.22	0.05	1.737	1.630	1.05
		18.80	0.05	1.522		
		20.81	0.40[a]	1.764	1.752	1.13
		20.03	0.40[a]	1.741		
		20.89	0.20[a]	1.706	1.706	1.10
		21.38	0.20[a]	1.707		

[a] Held overnight in water before measuring respiration rate.

24

Pink Salmon Alevins

Sublethal concentrations of tetrachlorocatechol caused the
rate of oxygen utilization by pink salmon alevins to increase.
The relative respiration rate of Sweltzer Creek pink salmon
alevins reached a maximum of about 1.5 between 0.175 and 0.250 ppm
tetrachlorocatechol (TABLE 7). At 0.150 ppm tetrachlorocatechol,
relative respiration rate dropped sharply to 1.16 and continued
to drop to less than unity at 0.125 and 0.100 ppm. At 0.050 ppm
tetrachlorocatechol, relative respiration rate rose to unity.
Relative respiration rates less than unity were possibly due to
experimental variation, in which case it appears that respiration
rate was not affected at tetrachlorocatechol concentrations of,
or below, 0.125 ppm.

Relative respiration rates of Skeena River stock alevins were
determined to be 1.33 and 1.35 in two trials at 0.25 ppm
tetrachlorocatechol (TABLE 7). These rates are less than the
value of 1.48 determined for Sweltzer Creek alevins and may have
been due to the fact that Skeena alevins were larger than those
from Sweltzer Creek. Trials M and N were conducted on successive
days using different individual fish from the same hatchery basket.
A sample of 20 fish from the basket was used to obtain the weights
report. lin TABLE 7 for these two trials.

The mean relative respiration rates of alevins were plotted in
FIGURE 3 where the trends in data already discussed can be seen
graphically. It can be concluded that respiration rate was increased
at concentrations greater than 0.125 ppm tetrachlorocatechol, but
that further research would be required to confirm the possible
decrease in respiration rate noted at lower concentrations of
tetrachlorocatechol.

25

TABLE 7 - Respiration rate of pink salmon alevins in tetrachlorocatechol (TCC); 15 alevins per 1,050-ml bottle, except where noted.

TRIAL AND TEMP. °F	STOCK	ALEVIN MEAN DRY WEIGHT, mg		CONC. TCC ppm	RATE OF OXYGEN UTILIZATION, mgO$_2$/hr/gm		
		body	Yolk		Individual Tests	Mean for Each Conc.	Relative Rate Expt./Control
F 40.5	Hatchery Incubated, Sweltzer Creek Race	26.50	27.46	Control	0.629	0.629	1.00
		26.50	27.82	Control	0.629		
		25.40	29.24	0.250	0.934	0.930	1.48
		25.70	29.07	0.250	0.927		
G 41.0		27.44	25.50	Control	0.700	0.684	1.00
		28.80	26.98	Control	0.668		
		27.35	25.27	0.175	1.085	1.042	1.52
		28.35	25.30	0.175	0.998		
H 40.8		31.39	23.65	Control	0.656	0.646	1.00
		34.39	23.92	Control	0.637		
		30.00	22.89	0.150	0.800	0.750	1.16
		32.40	23.14	0.150	0.701		
I 41.0		27.80	27.58	Control	0.743	0.774	1.00
		28.19	28.02	Control	0.805		
		29.20	26.69	0.125	0.689	0.730	0.94
		28.67	28.09	0.125	0.771		
J 40.8		29.80	23.23	Control	0.774	0.756	1.00
		30.40	23.56	Control	0.737		
		32.90	21.67	0.125	0.679	0.692	0.92
		30.50	22.46	0.125	0.704		
K 40.8		28.46	26.01	Control	0.613	0.646	1.00
		27.90	26.64	Control	0.678		
		28.25	25.08	0.100	0.520	0.615	0.95
		28.66	25.78	0.100	0.710		
L 41.0		27.24	26.37	Control	0.644	0.697	1.00
		27.98	24.88	Control	0.750		
		28.73	26.32	0.050	0.706	0.700	1.00
		28.28	27.41	0.05	0.694		
M[a] 40.8	Hatchery, Skeena Race	44.29[b]	11.53[b]	Control	0.855	0.855	1.00
		44.29	11.53	0.250	1.140	1.140	1.33
N[a] 40.8		44.29	11.53	Control	0.807	0.807	1.00
		44.29	11.53	0.250	1.092	1.092	1.35

[a] Ten alevins in 1,050-ml bottles.

[b] Body and yolk wieghts based on sample of 20 from M and N.

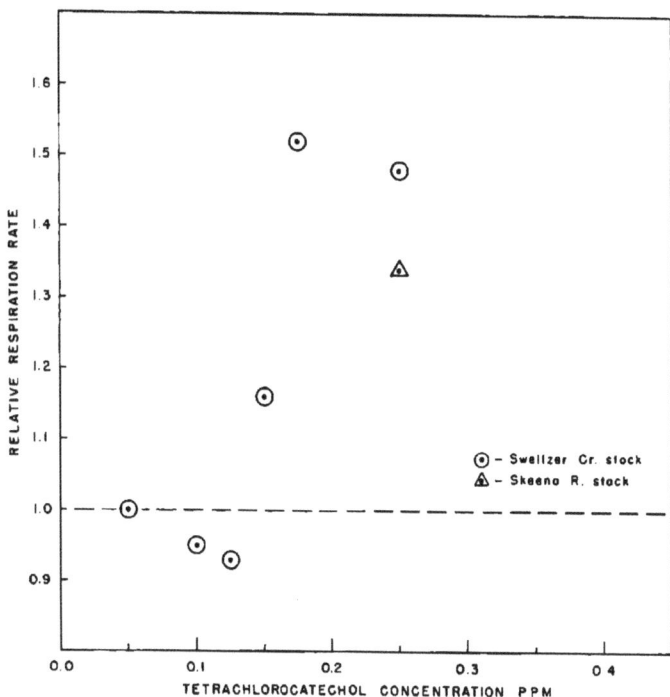

FIGURE 3 - Respiration rate (rate of oxygen utilization) of pink salmon alevins in tetrachlorocatechol relative to controls. Sweltzer Creek and Skeena River stocks, hatchery incubation.

27

Pink Salmon Fry

Respiration rates of newly emerged pink salmon fry from Sweltzer Creek incubation channel were measured at low concentrations of tetrachlorocatechol in an attempt to establish the minimum concentration at which tetrachlorocatechol influenced their respiration. Relative respiration rates varied at 0.175, 0.150 and 0.100 ppm tetrachlorocatechol. Results from Trials P and S showed a general trend toward increasing relative respiration rate with greater tetrachlorocatechol concentrations but data from Trials O and R failed to confirm such a trend (TABLE 8 and FIGURE 4). The difference may have been caused by the fact that fry in Trials O and R were held overnight in tetrachlorocatechol while fry in Trials P and S were not, but it is believed more likely that variations in fry activity were a primary cause of the variable results. Observations of pink salmon fry under conditions similar to those in the trials, except that light was not excluded, indicated that fry exhibited a high state of activity which was influenced primarily by behavior of individual fish rather than concentration of tetrachlorocatechol. Excitability during confinement may have been related to the fact that the fry were ready to migrate to the Fraser River estuary.

Although the data are not precise, results in FIGURE 4 suggest that tetrachlorocatechol caused an increase in respiration rate at concentrations greater than 0.10 ppm. It appears that respiration rate was unaffected at 0.05 ppm tetrachlorocatechol.

Biological Treatment for Oxidation of Chlorinated Catechols

A test of the ability of activated sludge to oxidize tetrachlorocatechol added to neutralized bleach waste (NBW) was conducted and a 96-hr bioassay used to evaluate treatment efficiency. After 24 hr of activated sludge treatment, neutralized bleach waste

28

TABLE 8 - Respiration rate of pink salmon fry in tetrachlorocatechol (TCC); five fry per 525-ml bottle.

TRIAL AND TEMP. °F	STOCK	FRY MEAN DRY WEIGHT mg	CONC. TCC ppm	RATE OF OXYGEN UTILIZATION, mg O_2/hr/gm		
				Individual Tests	Mean for Each Conc.	Relative Rate Expt./Control
0 51.0		36.77	Control	2.97	2.84	1.00
		37.59	Control	2.71		
		34.80	0.050	3.05	2.98	1.05
		34.58	0.050	2.91		
		35.93	0.025	2.71	2.74	0.96
		31.74	0.025	2.77		
P^a 44.0		57.60	Control	1.49	1.56	1.00
		63.58	Control	1.64		
		57.54	0.175	1.86	1.88	1.21
		40.80	0.175	1.90		
		63.25	0.150	1.55	1.59	1.02
	Incubation Channel, Sweltzer Creek Race	68.28	0.150	1.63		
		49.92	0.100	1.81	1.75	1.12
		67.64	0.100	1.69		
		60.31	0.050	1.52	1.61	1.03
		61.83	0.050	1.70		
		52.78	0.025	1.71	1.66	1.06
		47.01	0.025	1.61		
R 45.0		40.61	Control	1.63	1.66	1.00
		48.19	Control	1.70		
		45.92	0.175	1.81	1.74	1.05
		58.86	0.175	1.66		
		38.33	0.150	1.82	1.77	1.07
		51.93	0.150	1.72		
		55.20	0.100	1.52	1.56	0.94
		52.21	0.100	1.59		
		66.54	0.050	1.54	1.51	0.91
		53.04	0.050	1.48		
		62.47	0.025	1.65	1.66	1.00
		62.73	0.025	1.68		
S^a 45.6		44.72	Control	1.74	1.79	1.00
		48.85	Control	1.84		
		58.12	0.175	2.08	2.27	1.27
		30.57	0.175	2.46		
		51.66	0.150	1.91	1.94	1.08
		50.20	0.150	1.96		
		45.78	0.100	1.88	1.82	1.02
		56.32	0.100	1.77		
		40.86	0.050	1.83	1.78	0.99
		52.30	0.050	1.73		
		52.20	0.025	1.78	1.78	0.99
		57.15	0.025	1.78		

[a] Held overnight in water before measuring respiration rate.

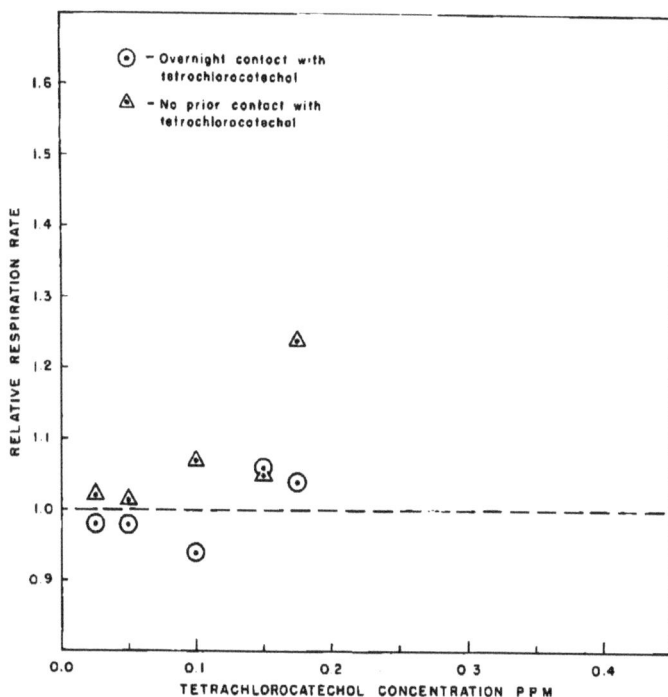

FIGURE 4 - Respiration rate (rate of oxygen utilization)
of pink salmon fry in tetrachlorocatechol relative to
controls. Sweltzer Creek stock from incubation channel.

plus 3 ppm tetrachlorocatechol (NBW+3TCC) was still toxic to sockeye fry at 40 per cent concentration (TABLE 9). Following five days of biological treatment, NBW+3TCC was non-toxic at 65 per cent concentration, the highest concentration bioassayed, indicating that biological treatment was apparently able to oxidize the tetrachlorocatechol molecule.

TABLE 9 - Toxicity of neutralized bleach waste (NBW) and NBW plus 3 ppm tetrachlorocatechol (NBW+3TCC), before and after biological treatment. Per cent mortality recorded during 96-hr bioassays of Pitt Lake sockeye fry (mean length 42 mm) held at 47°F.

CONCENTRATION OF WASTE BY VOLUME per cent	PER CENT MORTALITY				
	No Treatment	24-Hr Treatment		5-Day Treatment	
	NBW	NBW	NBW+3TCC	NBW	NBW+3TCC
90	-	40	100	0	-
65	-	0	60	-	0
40	-	0	40	-	-
30	100	-	-	-	0
20	20	-	-	-	-
15	0	-	-	-	-
0	0	0	0	0	0

The toxicity of NBW alone was reduced more quickly than that of NBW+3TCC. Before treatment, all test fish died at 30 per cent concentration of NBW and 20 per cent died at 20 per cent concentration (TABLE 9). Following 24 hr of treatment the waste was non-toxic at 65 per cent concentration, while 40 per cent of the fry died at 90 per cent concentration of treated NBW. After five days of treatment no mortalities occurred at 90 per cent concentration, the highest bioassayed. Sufficient NBW+3TCC was not available after five days to use a 90 per cent bioassay concentration, as used with NBW. However, since biological treatment apparently oxidized tetrachlorocatechol it is likely that 90 per cent concentration of NBW+3TCC would not have been toxic.

DISCUSSION

Acute Toxicity

Ninety-six Hour Exposure

The 96-hr TL_m of young sockeye salmon ranged between 0.7 and 1.3 ppm tetrachlorocatechol. Specifically, the 96-hr TL_m for natural smolts, freshly hatched natural and hatchery alevins, hatchery fry and incubation channel fry averaged about 0.8 ppm tetrachlorocatechol.

Furthermore, there appeared to be no difference in resistance to tetrachlorocatechol between Cultus Lake and Pitt Lake sockeye. On the other hand, advanced sockeye alevins were more resistant and had an average 96-hr TL_m of 1.2 ppm.

Differences in tolerance to tetrachlorocatechol of sockeye at various life stages may have been related to density of fish in the bioassay solutions, to the stage of development, or both. In some instances reported in the literature, apparent differences in tolerance have been caused by unequal densities of fish in the bioassay solutions in terms of grams of fish per liter. Katz and Chadwick (1961) found that at low densities of fish, mortalities occurred at low concentrations of toxicant (endrin), while high concentrations of toxicant were required to cause mortality at greater fish densities. On the other hand, Goodnight (1942) found that density of fish and temperatures within the normal range had no effect on toxicity of pentachlorophenol to several species of fish. Goodnight (1942) also reported that newly hatched lake trout alevins, Salvelinus namaycush, were more sensitive to pentachlorophenol than were juvenile fish. In the results reported herein, fish density did not appear to be the cause of the greater resistance of advanced alevins since they were tested at lower density (0.6 gm/liter) than were fry (2.0, 0.8 gm/liter) and smolts (3.9 gm/liter) as seen in TABLE 1. Freshly hatched alevins were bioassayed at a density of 0.3 gm/liter compared to 0.6 gm/liter for advanced alevins, but Goodnight's (1942) results with pentachlorophenol indicate that this difference in density would not have affected resistance of the newly hatched and advanced alevins. It appears likely, based upon the foregoing arguments, that freshly hatched sockeye alevins, fry and smolts were less tolerant of tetrachlorocatechol than were advanced sockeye alevins.

Pink salmon alevins and fry had 96-hr TL_m's of 0.29 and 0.26 ppm, respectively, and were less tolerant of tetrachlorocatechol than were sockeye. As an average it would appear that young pink

A 0.2 ppm concentration of dichlorocatechol caused no mortalities of sockeye alevins or fry during extended exposure. This concentration was less than one tenth of the 96-hr TL_m for dichlorocatechol.

The results indicated that a 31-day exposure did not cause mortality at significantly lower concentrations of di- and tetrachlorocatechol than did 96-hr exposure. However, it may not be possible to extrapolate these results to cover exposure to chlorinated catechols during the one year rearing period of sockeye in fresh water. The possibility of additional mortalities would depend upon several factors, especially detoxification mechanisms which the fish may possess, accumulation of toxicant in tissues, stress, and general condition of the fish (Graham, 1959; Mount, 1967).

Relative Toxicity and Effect of Chlorine and Hydroxyl Substitution

An indication of the relative toxic strength of di- and tetrachlorocatechol can be gained by comparison with acute toxicity of other substances, some of which are well known. Pentachlorophenate at 3 ppm was toxic to coho salmon in salt water within minutes (Alderdice, 1963). Pentachlorophenate and pentachlorophenol killed fathead minnows at concentrations between 0.32 and 0.35 ppm and silver-mouthed minnows at concentrations above 0.2 ppm (Crandall and Goodnight, 1959, Goodnight, 1942). The 96-hr TL_m's of sockeye fry to di- and tetrachlorophenol, reported herein, were 1.7 and 0.48, respectively. Phenol was toxic to several species of fish in the range from 10 to 20 ppm (McKee and Wolf, 1963). Catechol (pyrocatechol) was lethal to perch at concentrations from 5 to 12 ppm (Meinck, Stoof and Kohlschütter, 1956; Lucksteeg, Thiele and Stoltzel, 1955). The 96-hr TL_m of pumpkinseed sunfish to the insecticide Dieldrin was 0.0067 ppm (Cairns and Scheier, 1964).

34

Although various species of fish, which no doubt had different
tolerances, were used in obtaining the above results, some
generalized conclusions can be reached concerning relative toxicity
of di- and tetrachlorocatechol. Dichlorocatechol, it will be
recalled, was acutely toxic in the 2.0 to 2.7 ppm range while
tetrachlorocatechol was acutely toxic at 0.26 to 1.3 ppm. When
compared with toxicities of the several substances cited above it
is seen that chlorinated catechols were much less toxic than the
insecticide Dieldrin. On the other hand, the chlorinated catechols
were more toxic than phenol and catechol. These comparisons have
indicated that the chlorinated catechols had toxic strengths similar
to those of the chlorinated phenols: di-, tetra- and pentachlorophenol.
Chlorinated phenols have been responsible for destruction of fish life
in the past. Chlorinated catechols are potentially as dangerous.

Although comparisons indicated that toxicities of chlorinated
catechols and phenols were similar, there were small differences due
to chlorine and hydroxyl substitution which are worthy of discussion.
Toxicity in increasing order of the compounds tested was
dichlorocatechol, dichlorophenol, tetrachlorocatechol and
tetrachlorophenol. This order indicates that toxicity increased as
number of chlorine atoms on the molecule increased. Conversely,
toxicity declined as hydroxyl substitution increased from one to two
(e.g., tetrachlorocatechol less toxic than tetrachlorophenol).
However, decrease in toxicity caused by increasing number of hydroxyl
groups from one to two on the molecule was more than overcome by
increasing chlorine atoms from two to four (e.g., tetrachlorocatechol
more toxic than dichlorophenol). The results agree with general
observations by Sexton (1953) reported earlier and reemphasize the
significant role that chlorine substitution plays in increasing
toxicity of a molecule.

35

Sublethal Toxicity of Chlorinated Catechols

When discussing mechanism of toxic action it was suggested that chlorinated catechols may uncouple oxidative phosphorylation at acute and sublethal concentrations, as does pentachlorophenol. A symptom of uncoupling is increased rate of respiration or oxygen utilization (Negherbon, 1959, Goodnight, 1942) and the present experiments indicated that respiration was increased by di- and tetrachlorocatechol. Due to similarity of symptoms and chemical structure to pentachlorophenol it is reasonable to assume that chlorinated catechols are uncouplers. Similarly, it would be logical to assume that di- and tetrachlorophenol are also uncouplers.

Chronic exposure to chlorinated catechols or phenols at sublethal concentrations which cause abnormally high oxygen consumption may be to a fish's disadvantage. Since the chlorinated catechols and phenols apparently disrupt or reduce, by uncoupling oxidative phosphorylation, the flow of energy required for maintenance and growth, the fish would use its food less efficiently. Inefficient utilization of food over a long period would probably result in development of a smaller fish with less likelihood of successfully completing its life cycle.

It was shown that nearly lethal concentrations of di- and tetrachlorocatechol caused increased oxygen uptake, up to 1.5 to 1.6 times the control rate. On the other hand precise determination of a threshold concentration for respiration increase was not obtained. A threshold concentration is one at which a response is at the point of occurring and would become detectable following a slight increase in concentration of the toxicant. However, the data indicated concentrations at which a small response was detected and above which greater response was likely. These concentrations will be referred to as minimal and will be compared with 96-hr TL_m's in the following paragraphs.

36

The minimal concentrations affecting respiration of natural
and hatchery-reared advanced sockeye alevins were C.3 ppm and C.1
ppm tetrachlorocatechol, respectively. These concentrations were
approximately 25 per cent and 10 per cent of the 96-hr TL_m's
determined for these alevins. Reasons for the different degrees
of response were not apparent but may have been related to
experimental variation or some characteristic of the alevins. The
sockeye fry responded slightly to C.10 ppm tetrachlorocatechol
which was 12.5 per cent of the 96-hr TL_m for these fish.
Respiration rates of pink salmon alevins at 0.10 and 0.125 ppm
tetrachlorocatechol fell below those of the controls and it was
therefore difficult to estimate a minimal concentration. If
increase in respiration rate were the only criterion, it could be
estimated that the minimal concentration would be between 0.125
and C.15 ppm, or about 0.135 ppm. On the other hand, if the
observed decrease in respiration rate was caused by
tetrachlorocatechol at 0.10 ppm, then this would be the minimal
concentration at which a respiration response occurred. The
former value is about 46 per cent of the 96-hr TL_m and the latter
about 34 per cent. The minimal concentration of tetrachlorocatechol
for pink salmon fry was between C.10 and 0.150 ppm, or about
0.125 ppm, approximately 48 per cent of the 96-hr TL_m.

The preceding comparisons indicate that tetrachlorocatechol
interfered with normal metabolism of young sockeye, apparently by
uncoupling oxidative phosphorylation, at minimal concentrations
ranging from 10 to 25 per cent of the 96-hr TL_m and averaging
about 15 per cent. Interference with metabolism of young pink
salmon definitely occurred at minimal concentrations of 46 and 48
per cent of the 96-hr TL_m and possibly at 34 per cent.

It is interesting to compare the reported range of
concentrations over which another toxicant, Dieldrin, affected
respiration. Dieldrin, an insecticide which affects the central
nervous system, caused about an 18 per cent increase in oxygen

consumption of pumkinseed sunfish after exposure to a concentration which was 25 per cent of the 96-hr TL_m (Cairns and Scheier, 1964). No effect on oxygen consumption was noted at a Dieldrin concentration which was 11 per cent of the 96-hr TL_m. The relative levels at which sublethal effects of tetrachlorocatechol were obtained with sockeye alevins in the present study are in the same order of magnitude as noted for Dieldrin and indicate that some sublethal toxic effects may be readily noted at concentrations of tetrachlorocatechol ranging from 10 to 30 per cent of the 96-hr TL_m.

Respiration tests showed that young sockeye salmon were sensitive to tetrachlorocatechol over a wider range of concentrations than were young pink salmon. The opposite result might have been expected since, on the basis of acute toxicity, pink salmon were less tolerant than sockeye. Indications are that although general reactions of one species of Pacific salmon may be applicable to the other, specific results may not be. Therefore, proper consideration must be given to the sensitivities of each species when considering the effects of potential pollutants in specific locations.

Biological Treatment and Chlorinated Phenolic Compounds in Bleach Waste

Results have shown that tetrachlorocatechol was apparently oxidized by biological treatment with activated sludge. It can therefore be assumed that the less highly chlorinated catechols, mono-, di- and trichlorocatechol, would be oxidized as well, if present in bleach waste, as this reasoning was shown valid for the closely related chlorinated phenols (Ingols et al., 1966). Oxidation of tetrachlorophenol, if it exists in bleach waste, would also be very likely.

Toxicity reduction of NBW to which 3 ppm tetrachlorocatechol was added was slower than that of NBW. This difference in rate of toxicity reduction may have been caused by need for the biological

sludge to acclimate to oxidation of a higher concentration of tetrachlorocatechol than normally present in bleach waste or, possibly, to tetrachlorocatechol itself. In either case, the salient point is that chlorinated catechols apparently can be oxidized, and by proper design and operation, any one of a number of biological treatment systems with detention times ranging from hours to days could remove them.

As noted in the Introduction, the primary reason for studying toxicity of di- and tetrachlorocatechol was the expert opinion that they were likely constituents of bleach waste. Lapson and Anderson (1966) suggested that chlorinated phenols may represent some fraction of the organically bound chlorine in bleach waste. Therefore, there is reason to assume that chlorinated phenols as well as catechols may be present in bleach waste. Consequently the results reported herein regarding toxicity of di- and tetrachlorophenol (1.6 and 1.8 times as toxic, respectively, as the corresponding chlorinated catechol) take on added significance in consideration of bleach waste toxicity.

Laboratory results reported by Lapson and Anderson (1966) showed that substitution of some chlorine dioxide for chlorine during the first stage of pulp bleaching significantly reduced the amount of organically bound chlorine in the waste waters. In other words, toxicants such as chlorinated catechols and phenols might be eliminated by altering the bleaching process. Betts and Wilson (1966) have confirmed that substitution of chlorine dioxide for some chlorine during bleaching significantly reduced toxicity of bleach wastes. The use of chlorine dioxide in bleaching may become more significant in the future due to technical developments. However, for the present it appears that biological treatment will have to be relied upon to eliminate acute toxicity caused by organic compounds in bleach waste.

39

Potential for Toxic Conditions

Physical features of some watercourses are such that fish could evade toxicants if their senses alerted them in time. Goodnight (1942) determined that fish avoided high concentrations of pentachlorophenol but did not avoid lower concentrations which proved toxic. Due to similarities between pentachlorophenol, other chlorinated phenols, and chlorinated catechols, it is probable that fish would avoid only the higher concentrations of chlorinated phenols and catechols but not lower concentrations which might prove toxic.

Results and discussion have indicated that chlorinated catechols and phenols uncouple oxidative phosphorylation. Since these various chlorinated phenolic compounds apparently affect metabolism in a similar way it would be expected that a toxic situation could occur in a watercourse even though none of the individual compounds were at a toxic level. Studies of this type of situation (Herbert and Shurben, 1964) indicate that toxicities of some compounds are additive by using the equation $P_S/P_T + Q_S/Q_T = 1$, where P_T and Q_T are threshold concentrations of two toxicants and P_S and Q_S are concentrations to which the fish are exposed. For example, toxicity of phenol-zinc, zinc-ammonia, copper-ammonia and phenol-ammonia mixtures could be predicted from the equation (Herbert and VanDyke, 1964; Sprague and Ramsay, 1965). Supposedly the equation could be extended to include three or more compounds. According to Herbert and Shurben (1964), ammonium chloride and zinc sulphate mixtures suited the equation, but histological examination indicated that lethal concentrations of the two substances did not cause the same symptoms as lethal concentrations of only one of the toxicants. They therefore concluded that sublethal effects of each toxicant could sum within the fish and thereby kill it.

40

Recent research has indicated that sequential exposure to two different toxicants may predispose test fish to reduced tolerance of the second toxicant. Dugan (1967) found that exposure to sublethal concentrations of anionic detergents made test goldfish less tolerant when exposed later to the pesticides, Dieldrin and DDT.

The importance of chlorinated aromatic compounds as toxicants takes on additional significance in light of recent work by Ingols et al. (1966) who found that chlorination of sewage to reduce biochemical oxygen demand (BOD) or odor may produce highly toxic chlorinated compounds which are not easily oxidized by bacteria. Under these circumstances it is possible that chlorinated catechols or other chlorinated aromatic compounds may be formed during chlorination and discharged to waterways.

The foregoing discussion indicates that the toxicity results reported herein for chlorinated catechols and chlorinated phenols must be applied with care. Caution is especially necessary since pesticides, and chlorinated organics from sewage, pulp mills and other industrial operations may coexist or occur in sequence at various times in a watercourse. Therefore, consideration must be given to the combined acute and sublethal effects of toxicants, whatever the various sources, which may exist simultaneously or in sequence in a body of water.

CONCLUSIONS

1. Young pink salmon had about 35 per cent of the resistance of young sockeye to tetrachlorocatechol. Young pink and sockeye salmon were about equally tolerant of dichlorocatechol.

2. Advanced sockeye alevins were more tolerant of tetrachlorocatechol than were freshly hatched alevins, fry or smolts.

3. Thirty-one day exposure to di- and tetrachlorocatechol did not substantially increase acute toxicity.

41

4. Tetrachlorophenol was the most toxic of the compounds tested followed by tetrachlorocatechol, dichlorophenol and dichlorocatechol in descending order of toxicity.

5. Sublethal concentrations of di- and tetrachlorocatechol caused an increase in respiration rate which suggested that these toxicants were uncouplers of oxidative phosphorylation. Respiration rates of sockeye salmon alevins, and possibly fry, were increased at tetrachlorocatechol concentrations ranging from 10 to 25 per cent of the 96-hr TL_m. Respiration rates of young pink salmon were increased at tetrachlorocatechol concentrations of approximately 46 to 48 per cent of the 96-hr TL_m.

6. Generalized comparisons indicated that di- and tetrachlorocatechol and di- and tetrachlorophenol were much less toxic than insecticides such as Dieldrin, were more toxic than catechol and phenol, and of the same order of magnitude as pentachlorophenol.

7. Tetrachlorocatechol was apparently oxidized by biological treatment with activated sludge and it was presumed that other chlorinated catechols and phenols (except pentachlorophenol) would be oxidized as well, if present in bleach waste.

8. Due to possible synergistic effects it is recommended that consideration be given to the toxicity of combinations of chlorinated catechols, phenols and other toxic substances when examining a possible pollution problem.

42

LITERATURE CITED

Alderdice, D.F. 1963. Some effects of simultaneous variation in
    salinity, temperature and dissolved oxygen on the resistance
    of young coho salmon to a toxic substance. J. Fish. Res. Bd.
    Canada, 20(2): 525-550.

Betts, J.L. and G.G. Wilson. 1966. New methods for reducing the
    toxicity of kraft mill bleachery wastes to young salmon. J.
    Fish. Res. Bd. Canada, 23(6): 813-824.

Brannon, E.L. 1965. The influence of physical factors on the
    development and weight of sockeye salmon embryos and alevins.
    Internat. Pacific Salmon Fish. Comm., Prog. Rept. 12, 26 pp.

Brett, J.R. 1962. Some considerations in the study of respiratory
    metabolism in fish, particularly salmon. J. Fish. Res. Bd.
    Canada, 19(6): 1025-1038.

Bucksteeg, W., H. Thiele and K. Stoltzel. 1955. The effect on
    fish of toxic substances in waste waters. Von Wasser, 22, 194.

Cairns, J., Jr. and A. Scheier. 1964. The effect upon the
    pumpkinseed sunfish, Lepomis gibbosus (Linn.), of chronic
    exposure to lethal and sublethal concentrations of Dieldrin.
    Acad. Nat. Sci. Philadelphia, Notulae Naturae, No. 370, 10 pp.

Crandall, C.A. and C.J. Goodnight. 1959. The effect of various
    factors on the toxicity of sodium pentachlorophenate to fish.
    Limnol. Oceanog., 4: 53-56.

Dugan, P.R. 1967. Influence of chronic exposure to anionic
    detergents on toxicity of pesticides to goldfish. J. Water
    Pollution Control Federation, 39(1): 63-71.

Goodnight, C.J. 1942. Toxicity of sodium pentachlorophenate and
    pentachlorophenol to fish. Ind. Eng. Chem., 34(7): 868-872.

Graham, R.J. 1959. Effects of forest insect spraying on trout and
    aquatic insects in some Montana streams. Trans. Biol. Problems
    in Water Pollution, U.S. Dept. Health, Educ. Welfare, Tech.
    Rept., W60-3: 62-65.

Henderson, C. and C.M. Tarzwell. 1957. Bio-assays for control of
    industrial effluents. Sewage Ind. Wastes, 29(9): 1002-1017.

Herbert, D.W.M. and D.S. Shurben. 1964. The toxicity to fish of
    mixtures of poisons. I. Salts of ammonia and zinc. Ann. Appl.
    Biol., 53(2): 33-41.

Herbert, D.W.M. and J.M. Vandyke. 1964. The toxicity to fish of
    mixtures of poisons. II. Copper-ammonia and zinc-phenol mixture
    Ann. Appl. Biol., 53(6): 415-422.

43

Ingols, R.S., P.E. Gaffney and P.C. Stevonson. 1966. Biological activity of halophenols. J. Water Pollution Control Federation, 38(4). 629-635.

Katz, M. and G.G. Chadwick. 1961. Toxicity of andrin to some Pacific northwest fishes. Trans. Amer. Fish. Soc., 90(4). 394-397.

Malaney, G.W. 1960. Oxidative abilities of aniline-acclimated activated sludge. J. Water Pollution Control Federation, 32(12): 1300-1311.

McKee, J.E. and H.W. Wolf. 1963. Water quality criteria. 2nd ed. California State Water Quality Control Bd., Publ. 3-A, 548 pp.

Meinck, F., H. Stoof and H. Kohlschütter. 1956. Industrial waste waters. (Industrie-Abwässer). 2nd ed. Gustav Fischer Verlag. Stuttgart, 536, 48 D.M.

Mount, D.I. 1967. Considerations for acceptable concentrations of pesticides for fish production, pp. 3-6. In E.L. Cooper, (ed.), A symposium on water quality criteria to protect aquatic life. Amer. Fish. Soc., Spec. Publ., 4. (Suppl. to Trans. Amer. Fish. Soc., Vol. 96, No. 1).

Negherbon, W.O. 1959. Handbook of toxicology. Vol. III, Insecticides. W.B. Saunders Co., Philadelphia and London. 854 pp.

Rapson, W.H. and C.B. Anderson. 1966. Mixture of chlorine dioxide and chlorine in the chlorination stage of pulp bleaching. Pulp Paper Mag. Canada, 67(1). T47-54.

Sarkanen, K.V. 1963. Wood lignins, Chapt. 6. In B.L. Browning, (ed.), Chemistry of wood. Interscience Publishers, John Wiley and Sons, New York.

Servizi, J.A., E.T. Stone and R.W. Gordon. 1966. Toxicity and treatment of kraft pulp bleach plant waste. Internat. Pacific Salmon Fish. Comm., Prog. Rept. 13, 34 pp.

Sexton, W.A. 1953. Chemical constitution and biological activity. E. and F.N. Spon, Ltd., London. 424 pp.

Sprague, J.B. and B.A. Ramsay. 1965. Lethal levels of mixed copper-zinc solutions for juvenile salmon. J. Fish. Res. Bd. Canada, 22(2): 425-432.

Standard Methods for the Examination of Water and Wastewater, 1965. 12th ed. Amer. Public Health Assoc., Inc., New York. 769 pp.

White, A., P. Handler, E.L. Smith and D. Stetten, Jr. 1959. Principles of Biochemistry. 2nd ed. McGraw-Hill, New York. 1149 pp.